JUST LISTEN TO THIS
SONG I'M SINGING

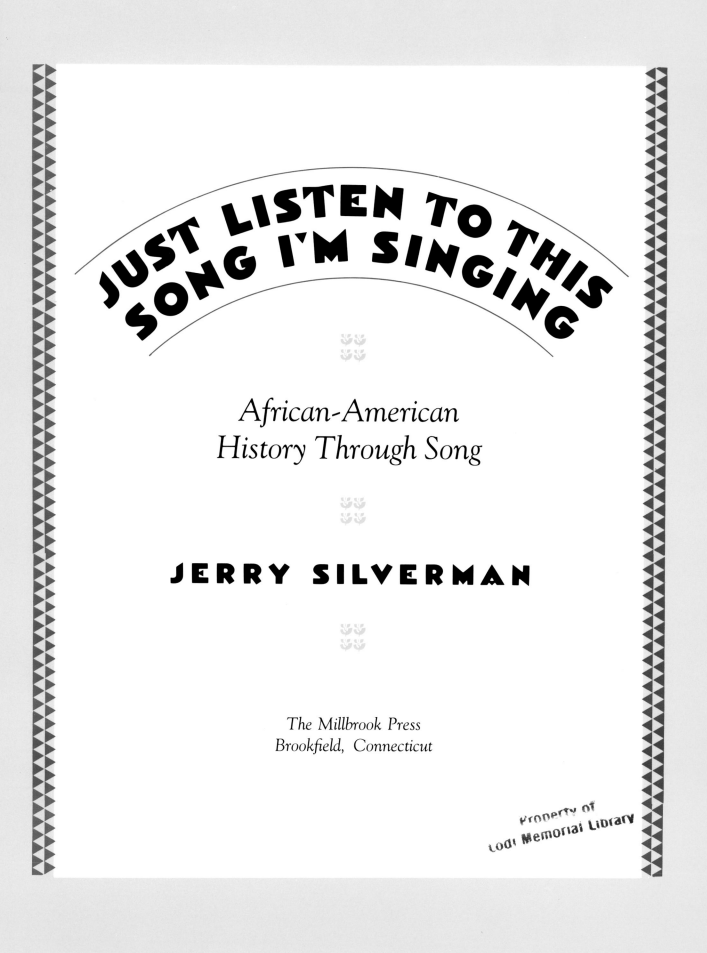

JUST LISTEN TO THIS SONG I'M SINGING

African-American History Through Song

JERRY SILVERMAN

The Millbrook Press
Brookfield, Connecticut

Photographs courtesy of Abby Aldrich Rockefeller Folk Art Center, Williamsburg,
Va.: p. 10; Bettmann Archive: pp. 12, 19, 34, 88; New York Public Library Picture
Collection: p. 18; The Schomburg Center, New York Public Library: pp. 23, 64,
80; The Museum of African American Art, Los Angeles, Palmer Hayden
Collection, gift of Miriam Hayden: p. 29; The Casey Jones Museum: p. 39; Frank
Driggs Collection: pp. 44, 56, 69, 75, 81; Lily Library, Indiana University at
Bloomington: p. 47; Chesapeake & Ohio Historical Society Collection: p. 54;
Archives Division–Texas State Library: p. 70; © 1978 Matt Heron: p. 87.

Library of Congress Cataloging-in-Publication Data
Silverman, Jerry.
Just listen to this song I'm singing : African-American history
through song / Jerry Silverman.
p.   cm.
Includes discographies, bibliographical references, and index.
Summary: Uses the music and lyrics of thirteen Afro-American songs
as a focal point for relating the history of the African-American
experience and for telling American musical history.
ISBN 1-56294-673-0 (lib. bdg.)
1. Afro-Americans—Music—History and criticism—Juvenile
literature.   2. Folk music—United States—Juvenile literature.
3. Folk songs, English—United States—Juvenile literature.
[1. Afro-Americans—Music—History and criticism.   2. Folk music—
United States.   3. Folk songs—United States.]   I. Title.
ML3556.S59   1996
782.42162'96073—dc20   95-22307   CIP   MN   AC

Published by The Millbrook Press, Inc.
2 Old New Milford Road, Brookfield, Connecticut 06804

Contents

JUST LISTEN TO THIS SONG I'M SINGING

Introduction

We are about to embark on a journey back in time to take a brief look at approximately one hundred years of African–American history—from the 1860s to the 1960s—as reflected in song. In those hundred years our country passed from being a slaveholding society, through a terrible Civil War, to becoming a nation where, in principle, "all men are created equal."

That true equality has not yet been attained is, unfortunately, a daily fact of life. Many of the songs in this book bear witness to the struggles of African Americans to achieve this equality. The music touched upon here includes spirituals, slave songs, work songs, blues, ragtime, and jazz. It concludes with a song from the civil-rights movement of the 1960s.

The first seeds of slavery were planted in 1619 when Dutch ships carrying black indentured servants arrived in Jamestown, Virginia. Although this marks the beginning of the saga of African Americans, written records of their music go back only a little more than one hundred years.

The reason for this is tragically simple.

We can be sure that the Africans who arrived here in the seventeenth and eighteenth centuries sang songs and told tales from their homelands, for they came from societies with oral musical traditions in which intricate choral and rhythmic ensemble singing and playing were highly developed. They sang songs of love, hunting, heroes, and battles. There were religious chants and lullabies. In short, they sang of the same human emotions that people feel the world over. However, because these people had neither written languages nor musical notation, these African musical creations were not preserved in written form, but rather were passed along from singers to listeners, from one generation to the next.

Once in America as slaves, the Africans must have sung frightening songs of the terrible ocean voyage and, as time went on, mournful songs of life in captivity. But their songs of yearning and despair, of

A group of slaves on a Charleston, South Carolina, plantation dancing to the accompaniment of the bones and a banjo. These instruments and dances were based on western African musical traditions.

bitterness and protest, fell on deaf ears. To our everlasting loss, seventeenth- and eighteenth-century plantations did not have resident musicologists, quill in hand, eager to transcribe and preserve this music. Even musically trained whites who may have come into contact with these songs probably reacted to them negatively. To their biased ears, the music would have been heard as incomprehensible, "savage" chanting, to be ignored at best, suppressed in many cases. Whites felt threatened when their slaves sang or otherwise expressed themselves in their native languages. After all, the owners thought, might not the slaves be plotting some uprising or escape?

It wasn't until well into the nineteenth century that the music of African Americans began to be recognized and appreciated outside of the black community. These spirituals (religious songs), work songs, and blues have been amply documented and collected. But in the more than two hundred years that had passed between the Africans' arrival in America and this awakening interest in their music, much was lost. The earlier songs had disappeared—vanished with their languages from the collective folk memory of the slaves.

When nineteenth-century white scholars began "discovering" the music of African Americans, they reacted with amazement and disbelief that such treasures could have existed for so many years all around them.

> The negroes keep exquisite time in singing . . . and will dash . . . through . . . a tune with wonderful skill. The best we can do . . . with paper and types . . . will convey but a faint shadow of the original. The voices of colored people have a peculiar quality that nothing can imitate; and the intonations and delicate variations of even one singer cannot be reproduced on paper.[1]

This remarkable passage is from the book *Slave Songs of the United States,* one of the earliest evidences of an appreciation of the music of the slaves outside of the black community. It was published 248 years after the first ship bearing human cargo docked at Jamestown, Virginia!

It took the Civil War and the end of slavery to bring the nation to the point where white scholars could begin seriously to accept the idea that there was a black culture in America worth studying and preserving.

We have come a long way since 1867, when *Slave Songs of the United States* took a first look at this music. In the coming pages we will discuss a song that was first published in that collection, as well as others drawn from the huge reservoir of the music of African Americans. We will examine how these songs reflect, and help us understand, some of the aspects of African–American history.

We will also examine how these songs influenced the development of American music as we know it today. This music would not exist if it were not for the contributions of generations of black musicians—men and women, famous and unknown. The music that comes from the souls of African Americans now belongs to us all.

On the surface, "Michael Row the Boat Ashore" reflects the quiet rhythm of the life of the island people, but the lyrics also tell a far more dramatic tale of escape from slavery to freedom.

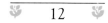

Michael, Row the Boat Ashore

My old parents didn't see these things—electric light, automobile, airplane. We come from rowboat time. Had to row from home to town and back. Sometime have to stay a whole day—have to wait on the tide—all that to row. . . .[2]

Stretching southward for some 300 miles (480 kilometers), just off the coast of South Carolina, from where the Santee River empties into the Atlantic Ocean to the mouth of the Saint Johns River in Florida, is a chain of low-lying islands called the Sea Islands. Most of the people who live on these islands are black and poor. They are the descendants of the old island cotton plantation slaves who, after the Civil War, acquired small pieces of land. For generations they have struggled—first as slaves, then as free citizens—to eke out a meager living from the sandy soil and the salt sea that surrounds them.

The islands include Folly, Edisto, Port Royal, and Johns off South Carolina; Tybee, Wassaw, and Sapelo off Georgia; and Amelia off Florida. Bridges between some of the islands and the mainland were not built until the 1930s. Even today many of the islands can be reached only by boat. As a result of this isolation, the life of the people has been relatively unaffected by the great changes that have taken place on the mainland.

Many aspects of the old slave culture and even older African traditions have been preserved, including the Gullah dialect. Gullahs are a West African tribe, and the name is also applied to the inhabitants of these islands. Many African words in Gullah have found their way into English, such as *cooter*, "tortoise"; *goober*, "peanut"; *gumbo*, "okra"; *juke* as in "jukebox."

As far back as the 1860s, the unique character of the people living on these islands was recognized, and the songs they sang were among the first songs of African Americans to be documented—written down and preserved. It was, in fact, during the Civil War (1861–1865) that three white scholars—William Francis Allen, Charles Pickard Ware, and Lucy McKim Garrison—began visiting the islands. They were so struck by the beauty and originality of the songs they heard there that they began collecting them and interviewing the singers to uncover the stories behind the songs.

It was they, who in 1867, published 136 of these songs in the book *Slave Songs of the United States*. They wrote in the introduction to the book: "The musical capacity of the negro race has been recognized for so many years that it is hard to explain why no systematic effort has hitherto been made to collect and preserve their melodies."[3]

The authors had gone to Port Royal Island on an educational mission in 1861. But they "were not long in discovering the rich vein of music that existed in these people."[4] How fortunate for us that the members of the mission recognized the great treasure that they had stumbled upon!

"Michael, Row the Boat Ashore" was one of the songs that found its way into that collection.

"Michael" is truly a rowing song, sung as the people (first as slaves, later as freemen) actually rowed back and forth from island to mainland, averaging twenty-four oar strokes per minute. It served to keep the oarsmen pulling together, ensuring as smooth a passage as possible. That's what the music did. But what about the words? As we will see here and throughout this book, the words to most of the songs can be read two ways: literally and "between the lines."

"Michael, Row the Boat Ashore" is full of Christian and biblical references. This is no accident, for ironically the slave owners felt it their "Christian duty" to convert the heathen (unbelieving) slaves into "good Christians." Apparently, the slave owners saw no contradiction between "love they neighbor" and "enslave thy neighbor." And the slaves themselves, by and large, accepted this new religion, with its promise of salvation, while often interpreting its teachings to fit their own needs and circumstances.

So it is that the "gospel boat" in the third verse lets us know that they consider themselves to be "true believers" in the preaching of Christ and his disciples.

In verse two, "Sister" is told to "trim the sail," to position it so that it catches the maximum amount of wind.

Verses four and five mention the Jordan River, a stream thousands of miles from the United States, which runs between the present-day nations of Israel and Jordan. Crossing the Jordan River meant entering the "Promised Land" (in biblical times called Canaan, the ancient name for Palestine, now Israel), as the ancient Hebrews did when they escaped from slavery in Egypt. It is this image—crossing the Jordan—that opens the second, deeper meaning of the song to us.

Slaves, whether they were ancient Hebrews enslaved by the Egyptians or nineteenth-century Africans enslaved by Americans, could not speak directly about their true feelings. A secret, symbolic, "coded" language had to be developed with which they could communicate with each other. The Promised Land of biblical times came to symbolize freedom to the black slave, as it had thousands of years before to the Hebrew slaves under the pharaohs of ancient Egypt.

Even "trimming the sail," which is something any sailor would say and do, could also mean: "Get ready—get in position to escape to freedom."

Finally, Michael is probably the archangel Michael who is mentioned both in the Bible and the Koran (the Moslem holy book) as the "great captain" (of the "gospel boat") who, sword in hand, slays the dragon (Satan, the devil) and helps the children of Israel (the biblical Hebrew "children"). In the early Christian church he is regarded as a helper of the church's armies against the heathen—all in all, a fitting symbol and inspiration for a boatload of slaves rowing the master's boat ashore.

▼▼▼

RECOMMENDED LISTENING

Each of the recordings listed here and in succeeding chapters under "Recommended Listening" contains the song discussed in that chapter, as well as a number of other interesting songs.

Harry Belafonte, *All-Time Greatest Hits.* RCA 6877.
Pete Seeger, *Children's Concert at Town Hall.* Legacy 46185.

MICHAEL, ROW THE BOAT ASHORE

Sister, help to trim the sail,
    Hallelujah!
Sister, help to trim the sail,
    Hallelujah!

Michael's boat is a gospel boat,
    Hallelujah!
Michael's boat is a gospel boat,
    Hallelujah!

Jordan's River is chilly and cold,
    Hallelujah!
Chills the body but warms the soul,
    Hallelujah!

Jordan's River is deep and wide,
    Hallelujah!
Meet my mother on the other side,
    Hallelujah!

If you get there before I do,
    Hallelujah!
Tell my people I'm coming too,
    Hallelujah! *Repeat Verse One*

Go Down, Moses

▼▼▼▼▼▼▼▼▼▼▼▼▼▼▼▼

The semi-secret references to freedom expressed in "Michael, Row the Boat Ashore" were transformed into an unmistakable cry for liberation in the spiritual "Go Down, Moses."

A spiritual, also called a Negro spiritual, is a heartfelt song with religious or biblical references. It is a song born out of slavery and oppression. Spirituals contain some of the most beautiful expressions of lyrical feelings to be found in any body of music.

The conditions under which spirituals were created could have inspired songs of hopelessness and despair, but instead the spirituals often offer hope—hope for a better life through faith and courage to face the trials of life because of that faith.

However, faith alone was not enough to overcome the bleakness and degradation that the slaves faced in their daily lives. Christianity, as taught in the white man's church, preached resignation and acceptance of suffering here on earth while promising eventual salvation in heaven. Those teachings may have satisfied the white "establishment," but they did little to alleviate the very real pain felt by blacks. They needed something they could relate to on a personal level, something that offered real hope. So while most slaves embraced the Christian faith, they brought many of its teachings "down to earth," to better relate them to their daily lives.

Echoing through the spirituals are lines such as: "You [God] delivered Daniel from the lion's den, so why not every man?" and "Joshua fought the battle of Jericho, and the walls came tumbling down."

The stories of Daniel (who was cast into a lion's den), and Joshua (whose victory at the battle of Jericho permitted the Hebrew "children" to enter the Promised Land) are found in the Old Testament of the Bible. The Old Testament begins with Genesis (the creation of the world) and goes on to recount how the people lived by the word of God through many trials and tribulations. There are many heroes in the Old Testament, but no one had a more significant story for black slaves than Moses.

It was the Israelite Moses who led his people out of slavery in Egypt and, after wandering for forty years in the desert, brought them

The story of Moses leading his people from slavery held great appeal for the slaves, who themselves wandered in the wilderness after emancipation.

up to the Promised Land. No more inspiring figure could have been found to give hope to the enslaved people in our country. It was Moses who stood before the Egyptian pharaoh and cried out, "Let my people go!" If it happened once, it could happen again.

The flight from Egypt by the Israelites is retold in the spring of each year by Jewish people at Passover, when families gather around a festive table to hold a seder, a symbolic feast and celebration of that memorable event. The story of Exodus (the flight) is retold, so that the people—particularly the children—should remember that "We were slaves in Egypt, and Moses brought us forth." Traditional songs are sung in Hebrew, but at some seders one song is sung in English as well: "Go Down, Moses." It is altogether fitting that this Negro spiritual, which sings of the universal desire for freedom, should be sung on this occasion.

▼▼▼

RECOMMENDED LISTENING

Roland Hayes, *Brother, Can You Spare a Dime.* Pearl 9484.
Paul Robeson, *Ballad For Americans.* Vanguard 117/118.

GO DOWN, MOSES

Thus saith the Lord, bold Moses said,
Let my people go,
If not, I'll smite your first-born dead,
Let my people go. *Chorus*

No more shall they in bondage toil,
Let my people go,
Let them come out with Egypt's spoil,
Let my people go. *Chorus*

The Lord told Moses what to do,
Let my people go,
To lead the Hebrew children through.
Let my people go. *Chorus*

O come along Moses, you'll not get lost,
Let my people go,
Stretch out your rod and come across.
Let my people go. *Chorus*

As Israel stood by the waterside,
Let my people go,
At God's command it did divide.
Let my people go. *Chorus*

When they reached the other shore,
Let my people go,
They sang a song of triumph o'er.
Let my people go. *Chorus*

Pharaoh said he'd go across,
Let my people go,
But Pharaoh and his host were lost.
Let my people go. *Chorus*

Jordan shall stand up like a wall,
Let my people go,
And the walls of Jericho shall fall.
Let my people go. *Chorus*

Your foes shall not before you stand,
Let my people go,
And you'll possess fair Canaan's Land.
Let my people go. *Chorus*

O let us all from bondage flee,
Let my people go,
And let us all in Christ be free.
Let my people go. *Chorus*

We need not always weep and mourn,
Let my people go,
And wear these slavery chains forlorn.
Let my people go. *Chorus*

Follow the Drinking Gourd

Sometimes the slaves would run away. Their masters was mean to them that caused them to run away. Sometimes they would live in caves. They got along all right—what with other people slippin' things in to 'em. . . . Some white people would help, too, for there was some white people who didn't believe in slavery.[5]

These are the words of an eighty-five-year-old ex-slave, Julia Brown, interviewed in 1937. About the same time, another ex-slave, Anthony Dawson (age 105) recalled how some white folks would "just pick up an extra nigger and show him where to get on de 'railroad system.' "

The "railroad system," known more commonly as the Underground Railroad, was a loose network of escape routes for runaway slaves headed north, primarily to Canada and freedom. It consisted of a series of "safe houses" and guides to lead the escapees from one refuge to another. The system reached from Kentucky and Virginia across Ohio, and from Maryland across Pennsylvania, through New York and New England. The risks for "conductor" and "freight" alike were great. Armed "paterollers" (patrollers) and their hounds would try to pick up the trail, with whippings, beatings, or worse in store for those unlucky enough to be caught.

It is difficult to know the exact number of slaves who reached freedom on the Underground Railroad from its beginnings in the 1840s until the Civil War. No precise records were kept. Estimates vary widely from about 1,000 to as high as 100,000. Whatever the number, however, the image of this "freedom road" captured the popular imagination of the time.

When the Civil War broke out, there was even a greater incentive to try to make the break for freedom. "I'll tell you how I runned away and joined the Yankees," recounted Boston Blackwell (age 98). "Abraham Lincoln declared freedom in '63, first day of January [the Emancipation Proclamation]. October '63, I runned away and went to

The Underground Railroad was not a railroad at all. Here escaping slaves transfer from a boat to a carriage on the perilous route to freedom.

Pine Bluff [Arkansas] to get to the Yankees. . . . When we gets to the Yankee camp all our troubles was over. . . . They told me I was free when I gets to the Yankee camp."[6]

Many songs of this period tell of the overwhelming desire to move up to "freedom land." In some of them the meaning is thinly disguised in "coded" language, with phrases that could have more than one meaning, depending on just who was listening ("Steal away to Jesus," "Get you ready, there's a meetin' here tonight," "I'm gonna cross over to the Promised Land"). In other songs there can be no doubt as to the message:

> When the sun comes back and the first quail calls,
> Follow the drinking gourd.
> For the old man is a-waiting for to carry you to freedom,
> If you follow the drinking gourd.

The "drinking gourd" is the group of stars known as the Big Dipper because of its shape. The handle of the "dipper" points north, north toward freedom.

The "old man" may have been an Underground Railroad conductor by the name of Peg Leg Joe. Joe, so the story goes, was a white sailor who had lost his right foot in an accident at sea, and had a wooden peg fitted in its place. He would travel from plantation to plantation near Mobile, Alabama, ostensibly looking for work as a handyman. Once hired, Joe would strike up acquaintances with many of the slaves, and soon he and the slaves would be singing this seemingly meaningless song. After a few weeks, Joe would hobble on to another plantation, where the same action would be repeated. He never returned to the same plantation twice, and he was never heard of again after his departure.

But come spring, "when the sun comes back and the first quail calls," slaves would start disappearing from the plantations that Joe had visited. Once safely into the woods, they carefully followed a trail marked by the imprint of a left foot and a round peglike mark in the place of a right foot. They followed the "mighty good road" of the Tombigbee River bank to where it joined with the Tennessee River. From there it was on to the Ohio River, forging ever northward to Canada and freedom.

Whether Peg Leg Joe himself led the escapees all the way, or passed them on to other conductors, we shall never know. We do know that there were many men, young and old, who risked their lives leading the escaping slaves north. There was also a woman, Harriet Tubman, herself a former slave, who made repeated trips to the South, bringing out an estimated three hundred people. Some called her "General" Tubman. To her people she was known as "Moses."

"Follow the Drinking Gourd" is a clear, unmistakable call to break with slavery once and for all.

▼▼▼

RECOMMENDED LISTENING

Richie Havens, *Songs of the Civil War*. Columbia 48607.
The Weavers, *Greatest Hits*. Vanguard 15/16.

FOLLOW THE DRINKING GOURD

Words and music by
Ronnie Gilbert, Lee Hays, Fred Hellerman, and Pete Seeger.
TRO © 1951 (Renewed) Folkways Music Publishers, Inc.
New York, N.Y. Used by permission .

The riverbank will make a very good road,
The dead trees show you the way,
Left foot, peg foot, traveling on—
Follow the drinking gourd. *Chorus*

The river ends between two hills,
Follow the drinking gourd,
There's another river on the other side,
Follow the drinking gourd. *Chorus*

Where the great big river meets the little river,
Follow the drinking gourd,
The old man is a-waitin' for to carry you to freedom,
If you follow the drinking gourd. *Chorus*

John Henry

▼▼▼▼▼▼▼▼▼▼

Can a man work faster than a machine doing the same job? Can a man swinging a 12-pound (5-kilogram) sledgehammer drive steel spikes into solid rock deeper and faster than a steam drill?

And if he does drive them deeper and faster, can he live to tell the tale?

In these days of super high-speed, computerized technology the answer to all these questions would certainly be no. But in 1873, in the Big Bend Tunnel of the C. & O. (Chesapeake and Ohio) Railroad Line near Talcott, West Virginia, the answer was by no means sure.

Digging a tunnel through a mountain had never been an easy job. The backbreaking task of hammering or drilling holes into solid rock, so that explosives could be inserted, had always been done by muscular men with heavy, long-handled hammers. The deeper the tunnel advanced under the mountain, the harder the job became. It got hotter, darker, harder to see, and harder to breathe. The danger of cave-ins increased. Premature explosions also took their toll in lives. An old song said it all: "There's many a man killed on the railroad and cast in a lonely grave."

The seemingly tireless workers who dug the tunnels, placed the wooden crossties, and laid the tracks for southern railroads during the period of great construction and expansion after the Civil War were almost all black men. Many had been slaves before the war. By 1873 the war was history, and they were free. But what did freedom really mean to millions of unskilled black men and women? Where could they go, and what could they do to earn their livelihoods?

Uneducated and largely unprepared for life in the "outside world," they found themselves at the very bottom of the postwar economic structure. This first generation of freed slaves and their children had only their strong bodies and their determination to offer potential employers. But even strength and determination, as we shall presently see, were often not enough.

For thousands of years, people had been dependent on wind, water, and domesticated animals for transportation and for help with many difficult tasks. Mills run by wind or water ground the grain; wind-

John Henry racing and beating the steam drill. But "he died with his hammer in his hand. . . ."

powered sailboats crossed the oceans; oxen plowed the land; horses pulled wagons and carried riders. But there was a limit to how hard, how fast, and how far these natural forces could work. Then, toward the end of the eighteenth century, a practical steam engine was developed.

The power unleashed by this miraculous invention transformed civilization as nothing had done before. What had previously been slow, tedious, often backbreaking labor now became almost a matter of shoveling in the coal and letting the steam-powered engine do the rest.

Industrial machinery, ships, trains—all powered by steam— caused a revolution in people's lives. It was called the Industrial Revolution. As a result, by the dawning of the nineteenth century, people could begin to travel faster and farther, and do more work more efficiently than ever before. As time progressed, more and more factories opened, mass-producing shoes, cloth, furniture, tools, and thousands of other things needed for an ever-growing population. A new breed of worker came into being—the factory worker. And when the steam-powered drill came to the Big Bend Tunnel in 1873, it seemed like the "sandhogs"—the tunnel workers—were about to be replaced by machinery.

When the captain (the foreman) announced one fine day that from now on the steam drill would take the place of the spike-driving men and their shakers (the men who held the spikes in place), one man said, "Hold on a minute! Let's see who can work faster."

So they had a race: Man against the machine.

Of all the hammer-swinging spike drivers that ever breathed rock dust underground, one man's exploits have echoed down to us through the years. They have survived in story and song, in folktale and legend. Often it is hard to separate fact from fiction, but one thing is for sure: John Henry was the meanest, leanest, keenest, swingingest, singingest, hammer-on-cold-steel ringingest spike driver that ever tore a hole through a mountain.

And this is his story.

▼▼▼

RECOMMENDED LISTENING

Big Bill Broonzy, *Big Bill Sings Folk Songs.* Folkways/Smithsonian 40028.
Merle Travis, *Bluegrass Spectacular.* C.M.H. Productions 15902.

JOHN HENRY

Hen - ry's ham - mer ring._____ You can ring._____

When John Henry was a little baby,
Sitting on his papa's knee,
Said, "That Big Bend Tunnel on the C. and O. Road,
It's gonna be the death of me." (2)

Well, the captain said to John Henry,
"Gonna bring me a steam drill 'round,
Gonna bring me a steam drill out on the job,
Gonna whup that steel on down." (2)

John Henry said to his captain,
"A man ain't nothin' but a man,
And before I let that steam drill beat me down,
I'll die with a hammer in my hand." (2)

John Henry said to his shaker,
"Shaker, why don't you pray?
'Cause if I miss this little piece of steel,
Tomorrow be your buryin' day." (2)

John Henry was driving on the mountain
And his hammer was flashing fire.
And the last words I heard that poor boy say,
"Gimme a cool drink of water 'fore I die." (2)

John Henry, he drove fifteen feet,
The steam drill only made nine.
But he hammered so hard that he broke his poor heart,
And he laid down his hammer and he died. (2)

They took John Henry to the graveyard
And they buried him in the sand.
And every locomotive comes a-roaring by says,
"There lies a steel-driving man." (2)

Joe Turner

One of the great contributions made by African Americans to American culture is the blues. It is at the root of jazz and almost all the American popular music that developed from jazz in the twentieth century.

Blues has an instrumental and vocal performing style and a melodic feeling that sets it apart from all other kinds of music. Hard times in life and love are the constant themes that run through the blues. A typical folk blues song consists of three-line verses, with the words of the first line repeated in the second line, and the third line completing the thought and the melody.

> I woke up this morning, feeling sad and blue,
> I woke up this morning, feeling sad and blue,
> My woman done left me—what am I gonna do?

This unusual three-line verse form was, and is, ideally suited to express the feelings of the singer. Since many blues were improvised (made up on the spot while the performer was actually singing) the repeated line—both words and music—gave the singer time to come up with the final phrase.

Blues began in the late nineteenth century as essentially vocal music. The first blues were generally sung without instrumental accompaniment, as were the work songs and spirituals. However, the guitar soon became the blues singers' main supporting instrument. Among the many advantages of the guitar is portability, which made it ideal for the many wandering musicians who flourished in the South toward the end of the nineteenth century and the first decades of the twentieth.

Often groups of musicians would gather and form little street bands. In addition to the guitar, these "combos" consisted of various combinations of other instruments: accordion, bass fiddle, jug, Jews'-harp, banjo, mandolin, harmonica, fiddle, and a variety of rhythm instruments, including washboard, bones, and all sorts of rattles, shakers, knockers, and scrapers.

They would play on street corners for whatever passersby might drop into their collection box. Dances, parties, and other social occa-

Prison guards supervising a convict work gang.

sions also brought in some money. It was, however, a very unsure and unpredictable way to earn a living. They never knew where and when the next engagement might take place. Often an unfriendly policeman or sheriff would tell the musicians to "move on."

In 1892, Pete Turney was elected governor of Tennessee. One of his first official acts was to give his brother Joe a job in the state prison system. It was Joe Turney's job to transport convicts from the Memphis jail to the state penitentiary in Nashville. Sometimes he took them to the prison farms along the Mississippi instead. Their "crimes," when indeed there were any crimes, were usually very minor, the arrests having been made to provide needed labor for the "farms."

The unfortunate prisoners were handcuffed together—eighty prisoners to forty links of chain—and marched through the streets of Memphis to the train station, where they boarded the train for Nashville. Those heading for the river farms were herded to the docks and taken by boat to their destinations.

It must have been quite an experience to see these long lines of men in their striped prison uniforms parading down the street, and to hear their shackles clanking as they shuffled along.

Joe Turney developed quite a reputation. He came to be called "the long-chain man." He was especially hated by the wives of the prisoners, because they knew that when he came to town, it was "bye-bye for some woman's man."

But he was paid the ultimate compliment. People began singing about him.

They sang, "They tell me Joe Turner's come and gone. . . ." A simple little song with three-line verses and a final line that didn't even rhyme with the first two: a blues.

As the song caught on, and verses were being created and sung by more and more people, his name changed slightly from Turney to Turner. That often happens in folk music, where the creators of a song don't bother writing it down, and other people sing what they think they heard.

According to W. C. Handy (whose life and composition, "Yellow Dog Blues" is discussed on page 55), who was living in Memphis at this time, this was the first blues he ever heard. That would make a good case for calling "Joe Turner" the "Granddaddy of the Blues."

▼▼▼

RECOMMENDED LISTENING

Mississippi John Hurt, *Last Sessions*. Vanguard 79327.
Big Bill Broonzy, *The 1955 London Sessions*. Collectables 5161.

JOE TURNER

*Chords in brackets may be omitted.

He come with forty links of chain.
He come with forty links of chain. (Oh, Lordy)
Got my man and gone.

They tell me Joe Turner's come and gone.
They tell me Joe Turner's come and gone. (Oh, Lordy)
Done left me here to sing this song.

Come like he never come before.
Come like he never come before. (Oh, Lordy)
Got my man and gone.

Casey Jones

Poor Casey Jones, he's dead and gone,
'Cause he's been on the cholly so long.

The expression "been on the cholly so long" means, "been a rambling railroad worker so long." And this song is a true story of a railroad worker, with a little fantasy, fiction, and folklore thrown in for good measure. In fact, it's such a good story, so full of high drama, human interest and tragedy, that it could easily form the basis for an exciting three-act play.

Cast of Characters
CASEY JONES, railroad engineer on the Illinois Central
SIM WEBB, Casey's fireman
JAY GOULD, railroad executive and financier
HELEN GOULD, Jay Gould's daughter

Place
Memphis, Tennessee, and along the
Illinois Central tracks at Vaughn, Mississippi

Time
The night of April 29–30, 1900

Act I
John Luther Jones, known as "Casey" for his hometown of Cayce, Kentucky, has just pulled his train into Memphis from Canton, Mississippi. It is 10:00 P.M., and Casey is ready to go home and go to bed. It has been a long run and he is tired. Just as he is about to leave the station he gets word that the engineer on the return run to Canton is sick. Casey offers to take his place. The train is due to leave at 11:00 P.M., but it is not until 12:50 A.M. that he heads engine number 382, pulling a six-car train, out of the South Memphis Yard with his black fireman Sim Webb in the cab, shoveling coal into the firebox. (Casey is white. In 1900, black men could work on trains as firemen and por-

ters, but not as engineers.) It is raining. Canton is 160 miles (257 kilometers) due south. He has been ordered to make up the lost time and get to Canton on time. Casey's long, drawn-out whistle is heard as No. 382 roars down the track at a mile a minute.

Act II

The scene shifts to Vaughn, Mississippi, 145 miles (233 kilometers) down the track from Memphis and 15 miles (24 kilometers) north of Canton. Casey has been making good time. It is about 4:00 A.M. and still raining.

Peering out of his window in the darkness, Casey sees every engineer's nightmare down the track. About 100 feet (30 meters) ahead, moving slowly off the main line onto a siding, is the tail end of a freight train. The freight crew knows that the delayed 11:00 P.M. from Memphis is due at any minute. They figure that they can move their slow freight out of the way in time to let Casey's "Cannonball" roar by.

What they don't figure on is Casey's 60-mile-(97-kilometer-) per-hour speed. Casey realizes in a flash that he will not be able to stop his train in time. He hollers at Sim Webb: "Jump, Sim, jump! Save yourself, we ain't gonna make it!" Sim jumps for his life. The last thing Sim hears before the crash is the long, mournful whistle of old 382.

Act III

The story of the wreck is telegraphed around the nation. Casey's body is found in the wreck with one hand on the brakes and the other on the whistle cord. Sim Webb is interviewed. Pictures, sketches, and diagrams appear in newspapers from coast to coast. Casey's heroism is praised: "He could have jumped, too, but he chose to stay with it, hoping to avert the crash." The "folk process" takes over. Songs are written. Names, places, and dates are changed. People who have nothing to do with the actual event have their names inserted into some of the songs.

This epic tale of a white engineer and his black fireman inspired songwriters, both white and black, across the nation. Sometimes it is not possible to label a song as "white" or "black." What is certain about "Casey Jones" is the fact that singers of both races picked up the story, varied the tune, and changed, added, and subtracted verses.

Sim Webb, Casey's engineer, spent his life telling and retelling the story of Casey Jones. He died in 1957 at the age of 83.

Epilogue

Jay Gould (1836–1892) was one of the major railway financial speculators of the nineteenth century. He and some of his cronies were called "robber barons" because of their ruthless and sometimes shady methods of doing business. He controlled numerous railways, including the Erie and the Union Pacific. By 1880 he was in virtual control of 10,000 miles (16,000 kilometers) of railway, about one ninth of the railway mileage of the United States at that time. His daughter Helen (1868–1938) became widely known as a philanthropist for her gifts to American army hospitals during the Spanish-American War (1898) and for her many contributions to New York University. Neither she nor her father had anything to do with the Illinois Central Railroad or with Casey Jones.

This is the way it often is with "factual" folksongs. As the years go by, memories fade and other "facts" creep in. This might disturb the historians, but not the songwriters and singers, who are only interested in a good song. And this is a good song.

Sim Webb got up and dusted himself off after his famous jump, and went back to railroading. He never forgot that awful night, telling and retelling the story over the years to anyone who would listen.

▼▼▼

RECOMMENDED LISTENING

Furry Lewis, *Shake 'Em On Down.* Fantasy 24703.
Sidney Bechet, *Bechet! The Legendary Sidney Bechet.* GNP/Crescendo 9012.

CASEY JONES

Casey Jones was a good engineer,
He told his fireman not to fear,
All he needed was water and coal;
Put your head out the window, see the drivers roll.
Drivers roll, drivers roll,
Put your head out the window, see the drivers roll.

When we got within a mile of the place,
Old Number One stared us right in the face;
The conductor pulled his watch, and mumbled and said,
"We may make it but we'll all be dead.
All be dead, all be dead,
We may make it but we'll all be dead."

As the two locomotives was about to bump
The fireman prepared to make his jump;
The engineer blowed the whistle, and the fireman bawled,
"Please, Mr. Conductor, won't you save us all?
Save us all, save us all,
Please, Mr. Conductor, won't you save us all?"

O ain't it a pity, ain't it a shame?
The six-wheel driver had to bear the blame.
Some were crippled, and some were lame,
And the six-wheel driver had to bear the blame.
Bear the blame, bear the blame,
And the six-wheel driver had to bear the blame.

Jay Gould's daughter said before she died:
"There's one more road I'd like to ride."
"Tell me, daughter, what can it be?"
"It's the Southern Pacific and the Santa Fe.
Santa Fe, Santa Fe
It's the Southern Pacific and the Santa Fe."

Jay Gould's daughter said before she died,
"Father, fix the blind so the bums can't ride;
If ride they must, let them ride the rod,
Let 'em put their trust in the hands of God.
Hands of God, hands of God,
Let 'em put their trust in the hands of God."

The Ragtime Dance Song

What is . . . called ragtime is an invention that is here to stay. That is now conceded by all classes of musicians.[7]

These words were written in 1908 by Scott Joplin in the introduction to his *School of Ragtime* piano exercises. He was attempting to defend the reputation of a "new" kind of music with which his name was closely associated. He went on to say: "Syncopations are no indication of light or trashy music, and to shy [throw] bricks at 'hateful ragtime' no longer passes for musical culture."[8]

Scott Joplin (1868–1917) is a name with which every American music lover should be familiar. He, more than any of his contemporaries, took this new music called ragtime out of its somewhat shady beginnings and presented it on the world stage. When he used the term "hateful ragtime," he was reacting to many white music critics of the day who found this music unappealing, unappetizing, and even uncivilized, even though the public loved it. Almost every composer through the ages who has come up with something new and original has been faced with similar criticism.

The driving force behind ragtime music is that word, "syncopation." Syncopation is so much a part of the music we hear all around us that we are generally not even aware of it. The best way to arrive at a definition of syncopation is to begin by examining what it is *not*.

When you hear a band leading a parade down the street and see the marching feet coming down exactly in time to the music—"one-two-three-four . . . left-right-left-right . . ."—you are enjoying *unsyncopated* music. A musician would say that everything is squarely "on the beat."

Now, imagine that same parade, but this time the feet come down "one-two . . . four . . . left-right . . . left." That would surely "mess up" the parade! Leaving out a beat is one example of syncopation. Another kind of syncopation might be squeezing in a beat between two other beats. You couldn't march too well to that either. But

Scott Joplin was by far the most famous ragtime composer and pianist of his day.

that's just fine, because ragtime music is not marching music—it's dancing music. Ragtime music is full of syncopated rhythm, accented (strong) beats that catch the listener by surprise. That is what gives ragtime its characteristic and appealing sound.

This change from the familiar, comfortable "one-two-three-four" (originally called "ragged time," then "rag time" and finally "ragtime") shook up the musical world in the 1890s and early 1900s. Musical advances and changes have always caused people to long for "the good old days," and to say, "They don't write 'em like they used to." So Scott Joplin spent much of his time and energy trying to justify the value of his music to the music "establishment," while, at the same time, enjoying a measure of popular success.

Despite the fact that Joplin, and other black ragtime composers, such as Benjamin R. Harney ("You've Been a Good Old Wagon But You Done Broke Down"—the first ragtime song ever to appear in print, in 1895) and Will Marion Cook ("Who Dat Say Chicken in Dis Crowd?") had been laying the groundwork in the 1890s for the ragtime "explosion" that was to sweep the nation around the turn of the century, it was John Philip Sousa, a white composer ("The Stars and Stripes Forever"), arranger, and bandleader who first introduced ragtime to a broad audience of Americans. It was at the 1904 World's Fair in St. Louis, Missouri, that Sousa's symphonic band tore its way through foot-tapping arrangements of cakewalks and rags to enthusiastic, mostly white, audiences. Sousa followed up his success at St. Louis with many national tours in which ragtime music was an integral part of his program.

Scott Joplin was born on November 24, 1868, in Texarkana, Texas, just five years after his father, a slave, had been set free. His mother had been free from birth. The Joplin home was full of music. His parents played the violin and the banjo, and he and his brothers and sisters were encouraged to study music as well.

At the age of seven Scott began experimenting on a neighbor's piano, and by the age of eleven his piano playing was the talk of the black community. He studied for a while with a German "professor" in Texarkana, who helped him organize his self-taught musical skills into a more formal system.

In 1882, when Scott was fourteen, he left home to try his luck as an itinerant musician. Despite his tender age, he found work in saloons and bordellos in Texas, Louisiana, Missouri, Arkansas, and Kansas.

It was while on this "circuit" during the 1880s that Scott began hearing, and soon creating, this new, rhythmically appealing, as yet unnamed music that would come to be known as ragtime.

Most of Joplin's rags, as well as those of his contemporaries, were written for the piano. The composition of his that first brought him recognition in 1899, is 'The Maple Leaf Rag,' named in honor of a social club in Sedalia, Missouri, where he was performing. A few years later, when his reputation had been established, the *St. Louis Globe-Democrat* had these somewhat peculiar words to say in his praise on June 7, 1903: ". . . a composer of music, who despite the ebony hue of his features [!!!] and a retiring disposition, has written possibly more instrumental successes than any other local composer. . . . His first notable success . . . was the 'Maple Leaf Rag,' of which thousands and thousands of copies have been sold."

Joplin's piano rags are short, lively instrumental compositions of four or five sections, lasting just a few minutes. He wanted very much to expand his musical horizons and compose more ambitious music—a sort of folk ballet based on the popular dances of the day. His publisher resisted the idea, so Joplin financed a public performance of the *Rag Time Dance* himself. In this way he hoped to convince the publisher of the value of the project.

The publisher was not persuaded, but did publish a condensed version of the musical score. The "Rag Time Dance Song" is part of that score.

The lyrics to this song give us a good picture of how songwriters expressed themselves in the first years of the twentieth century.

Many ragtime songs are about dances, balls, and parties—that is, about ragtime itself. People are always dressed in their fanciest clothes. The men are handsome, the women are "belles." In this song the point is made that the "hall was illuminated by electric lights," which was still a novelty in those days.

Joplin choreographed (created and directed) the dance steps himself. The "cakewalk prance" (prance was *the* favorite word of the time to rhyme with dance) refers to a fancy dance contest in which the winning couple was awarded a big chocolate cake.

Joplin had even greater musical plans than expanding his rags into a ballet. On June 7, 1903, the St. Louis *Globe-Democrat* reported: "Joplin's ambition is to shine in other spheres. . . . To this end he is . . . toiling upon an opera . . . which he hopes to give an early production in this city."

That opera, *Treemonisha,* based on African–American folk themes, was never produced in Joplin's lifetime, except for one performance Joplin staged himself, with his own piano accompaniment. If his publisher had objected to publishing a 9-page *Rag Time Dance* ballet, the possibility of publishing a 230-page operatic score was completely out of the question. And even if it were to be published, who would

An elegantly attired couple doing the Rag Time Dance as pictured on the cover of the original 1906 sheet music. The price was 75 cents.

finance its production? What theater would present it? Who would come to see it?

These were very real questions in 1903, and for many years thereafter. White theater managers and audiences were not ready to support serious music by black composers. While it was all right for a black man to write little ragtime pieces, an opera was out of the question!

While continuing to compose successful rags, Joplin struggled futilely to get *Treemonisha* produced. He scraped together the money to publish the score himself in 1911, but a promised 1914 production in a theater in Harlem was canceled when the theater's management felt that musical comedies would make more money.

Joplin was devastated by this turn of events. His health rapidly deteriorated, and he died on April 1, 1917, at the age of forty-nine.

In January 1972 the music department of Morehouse College in Augusta, Georgia, and the Atlanta Symphony revived the long-forgotten opera in Atlanta. Then, in May 1975, the Houston Grand Opera presented *Treemonisha* in a full-fledged professional production. Later that year the work was presented in New York—on Broadway! It was a rousing success.

The 1970s witnessed a tremendous revival of the popularity of ragtime music in general and Joplin's compositions in particular. The movie *The Sting* contributed to this ragtime revival by featuring Joplin's rag "The Entertainer" in its soundtrack.

Ragtime music was and is "in the air—you can't escape it 'cause it's everywhere!"

▼▼▼

RECOMMENDED LISTENING

Scott Joplin, *The Entertainer*. Biograph BCD 101. Piano only, no vocal.
Jerry Silverman, *The Ragtime Songbook*. Cassette accompanying the book of the same name. See *Further Reading*, page 93.

THE RAGTIME DANCE SONG

Words and Music by Scott Joplin

"Do not play this piece fast. It is
never right to play 'rag-time' fast."
—Scott Joplin

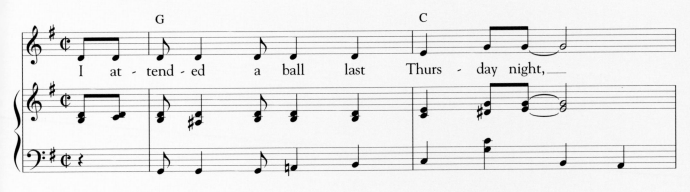

I at-tend-ed a ball last Thurs - day night,

giv - en by the down - town swells. Ev - 'ry man came out__ in full

dress al - right, And the girls were so - ci - e - ty belles. The

hall was il - lu - mi - na - ted by e - lec - tric lights, It

cer - tain - ly was a sight to see. So man - y sport - in' folks there with -

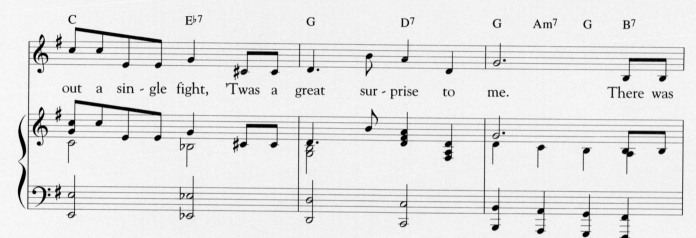

out a sin - gle fight, 'Twas a great sur - prise to me. There was

lit - tle Sam Smith, the great la - dies' man, Who had the

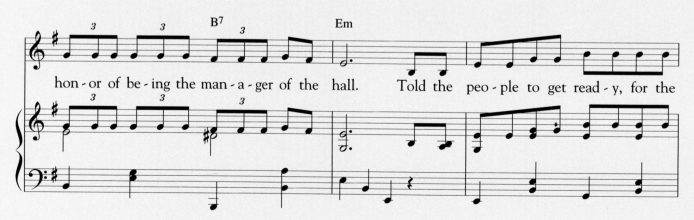

hon - or of be - ing the man - a - ger of the hall. Told the peo - ple to get read - y, for the

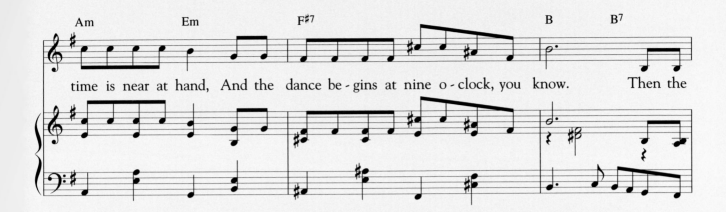

time is near at hand, And the dance be - gins at nine o - clock, you know. Then the

or - ches - tra be - gan to play the sweet en - tranc - ing mu - sic of the

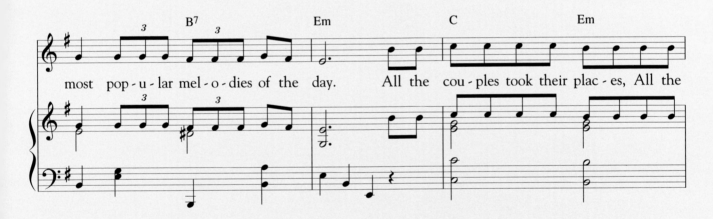

most pop - u - lar mel - o - dies of the day. All the cou - ples took their plac - es, All the

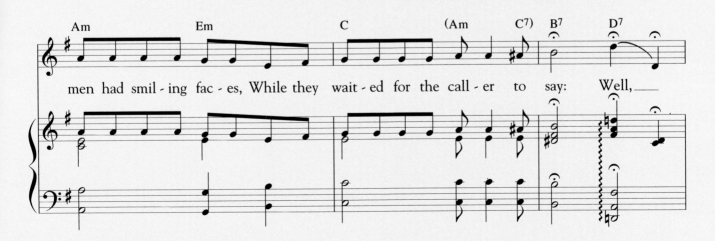

men had smil - ing fac - es, While they wait - ed for the call - er to say: Well,___

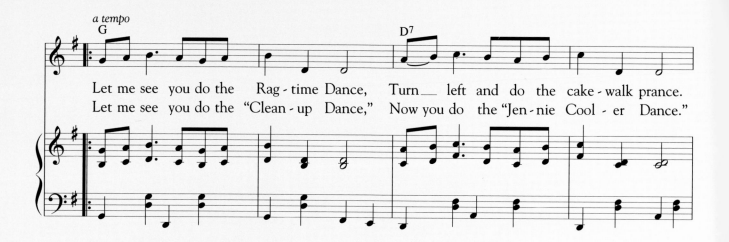

Let me see you do the Rag - time Dance, Turn___ left and do the cake - walk prance.
Let me see you do the "Clean - up Dance," Now you do the "Jen - nie Cool - er Dance."

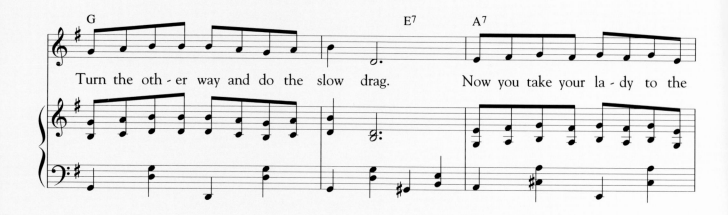

Turn the oth - er way and do the slow drag. Now you take your la - dy to the

World's Fair; And do the Rag - time Dance. Dance.

Yellow Dog Blues

▼▼▼▼▼▼▼▼▼▼▼▼▼▼▼▼▼▼

The Yazoo Delta Railroad tracks cross the Southern Railroad Line tracks at Morehead, Mississippi.

A gang of black section hands is hard at work under a blistering summer sun, straightening the rails that have expanded in the furnacelike heat. On the Yazoo line, a locomotive is slowly following the progress of the men. The letters "Y.D." are painted on its coal car. As the men sweat and strain, prying the buckled rails back into alignment with long crowbars, a voice is heard singing softly, "Goin' where de Southern cross de Yaller Dawg." The Yaller Dawg—The Yellow Dog—that's what the men call the Yazoo Delta.

The refrain is picked up by a wandering blues guitarist, who adds some more words and a couple of chords. The song travels with the bluesman in his dusty wanderings. One day in 1903, in nearby Tutwiler, a trained black musician hears it and, as is his custom, jots it down in his notebook.

William C. Handy (1873–1958) was born in Florence, Alabama, on November 16, 1873. His parents were among the four million slaves who had been freed and left to shift for themselves after the Civil War.

As young Will grew he became increasingly fascinated by the sounds of music he heard all around him. Once, he secretly saved up his pennies and nickels to buy a guitar. When he finally bought it, his father, a preacher, was outraged.

"A box! A guitar! One of the devil's playthings. Take it away. Take it away, I tell you. Get it out of your hands. Whatever possessed you to bring a sinful thing like that into our Christian home? Take it back where it came from."[9]

Although the guitar was returned—actually exchanged for a *Webster's Unabridged Dictionary*, which his father thought would do him good—Will was more determined than ever to learn to play an instrument.

When he entered high school he secretly obtained a cornet and began studying with a musician who had recently arrived in town from

Track workers on the C.&O. (Chesapeake and Ohio) Railroad in the 1890s. Rhythmic work songs helped coordinate the men's movements.

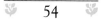

Memphis. Not only did Will learn to play the cornet from this man, but he heard fascinating stories about the music and the good times in Memphis.

By the time father Handy found out what his son was up to, it was too late to do anything about it. Will began playing for dances in a local band. He was, and would remain, a musician.

However, since there was still no sympathy at home for any thought of a musical career, he tried his hand at various occupations. He taught public school for two years in Florence before going off to Birmingham to work in a steel-pipe factory. When the economic panic of 1893 closed down the factory, Handy knew what he must do. He had continued with his music as a sideline, but now he was resolved to dedicate his life exclusively to music.

For the next ten years he lived the life of a traveling musician, playing with various bands in big cities like Chicago and St. Louis, smaller towns like Evansville, Indiana, and Henderson, Kentucky, and as far south as Clarksdale, Mississippi.

It was sometime during his Clarksdale period (1903) that Handy heard an unknown blues guitarist singing something about "Goin' where de Southern cross de Yaller Dawg." He was struck by the beauty of the melody and the descriptiveness of the words. After copying down the song without really knowing what he might do with it, he turned his attention to what really had been his goal all along: moving to Memphis, where there was a great demand for music.

By 1905 he was already a part of the "Memphis scene," leading his band, the Handy Band, at many of the dances and social events taking place nightly around the city. He even became involved in politics, composing his first big hit in 1909, "Memphis Blues," as a campaign song for Edward H. Crump, a well-known Memphis politician who was running for mayor. Crump won the election, and Handy was on his way!

In 1914, Handy wrote his most famous song, "St. Louis Blues." It took the country by storm, much as Scott Joplin's "Maple Leaf Rag" had done fifteen years earlier.

> I got the St. Louis blues, just as blue as I can be,
> That man's got a heart like a rock cast in the sea,
> Or else he wouldn't have gone so far from me.

Now it was time to dust off the old "Yellow Dog Blues."

W. C. Handy's love of music begin at an early age. Here he is shown in his high school band uniform, holding his beloved cornet.

Here is how Handy recalls the moment in his autobiography, *Father of the Blues:*

I undertook to answer the question raised by Shelton Brooks in his remarkable hit, "I Wonder Where My Easy Rider's Gone" [1913]. The country had gone stark, raving mad over the sweet-loving jockey with the easy ways and the roving disposition. I proposed to pick up Susan Johnson and Jockey Lee, Brooks's characters, in a parody of the original lyric, locating the lost rider "down where the Southern cross' the Dog."[10]

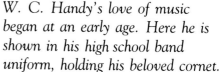

In Brooks's song, Miss Susie Johnson bets all her money on a horse ridden by her "easy rider," who disappears before the race—with the money. But she still loves him (poor girl!).

> I'd put all my junk in pawn,
> To bet on any horse that jockey's on.
> Oh, I wonder where my Easy Rider's gone.[11]

Finding the three-line folk blues original too restrictive musically, he expanded the form to suit the popular musical taste of his time. Handy was able to combine the traditional elements and his own inspiration into an original masterpiece. That was his genius.

W. C. Handy continued writing his popular blues-based compositions for many years. When he died in New York City on March 28, 1958, about 150,000 people jammed the streets of Harlem to say good-bye to the "Father of the Blues."

Just as Joe Turney's name got changed to Joe Turner, so did Handy change the name of Brooks's "sweet-loving jockey" from Sammy Green to Lee.

Then Handy paints a long descriptive section of life in the rural South as Miss Susan Johnson waits unhappily for her man to reappear. He refers to "Bam" (Alabama), "Old Beck an' Buckshot land" (common names for hunting hounds), and the boll weevil (the cotton-eating insect that devastated the South's economy for many years). Finally, good news arrives in the chorus: "Dear Sue, your Easy Rider struck this burg today."

▼▼▼

RECOMMENDED LISTENING

Louis Armstrong, *Louis Armstrong All Stars.* Storyville 4012.
Bessie Smith, *The Complete Recordings, Vol. 2.* Legacy 47471.

YELLOW DOG BLUES

Words and Music by W.C. Handy

1. E'er since Miss Su - san John - son lost her Jock - ey, Lee, ___ There has been
2. I know the Yel - low Dog Dis - trict ___ like a book, ___ In - deed I

much ex - cite - ment, more to be; ___ You can hear her moan - ing night ___ and
know the route that Rid - er took, ___ Ev - 'ry cross - tie bay - ou, burg ___ and

but the hike __ ain't far. _____ He's __ gone where the South - ern

cross' __ the Yel - low Dog. _____ Dear Sue, your __

The Long-Line Skinner Blues

▼▼▼▼▼▼▼▼▼▼▼▼▼▼▼▼▼▼▼▼▼▼▼▼▼▼▼▼▼

Well, it's good morning, captain. Good morning, shine,
And it's good morning, captain. Good morning, shine.
Do you need another mule skinner out on your new road line?

Before trucks and tractors did all the heavy hauling, beginning about 1900, that work was done by wagons drawn by mules, sometimes as many as eight pairs hitched together, driven by a vanished breed of men—the mule skinners.

They got to be called mule skinners because they were so skillful with their long whips that they could flick a piece of skin off the backside of any of their sixteen mules if that animal showed signs of slowing down.

The above conversation between the captain (the man who did the hiring) and "shine," (the black would-be skinner) is in the typical three-line folk blues format: one repeated line and a conclusion in the third line. The skinner looking for work tries to convince the boss that he is, indeed, the man for the job.

I like to work, I'm rollin' all the time,
I like to work, I'm rollin' all the time.
I can carve my initials right on a mule's behind.

Mule skinners were tough characters. They had to be. The work was hard, the hours were long, the pay was low.

I'm workin' on the new road for a dollar and a dime a day,
I'm workin' on the new road for a dollar and a dime a day,
Give my woman the dollar and throw the dime away.

All of the above verses are from a traditional song called "Mule Skinner Blues." By the time we get to "Long-Line Skinner," our man has gotten his job and is boasting about his drinking as well as his skinning. "Long-Line Skinner" is also a blues. The three-line verse with the repeated line has been reshaped into a one-line verse and a two-line chorus, but musically it covers the same ground—the same number of measures (twelve) and the same chords as "Mule Skinner Blues."

A mule skinner hauling a load of cotton to market. Each bale weighed 500 pounds.

In verse three, the line "I'm down in the bottom . . ." refers to the rich, fertile land along the river, also called bottomland. That's where crops like sugarcane grow the best. Sometimes the heavily laden wagon would sink to its hub caps in the soft ground. The skinner would curse his mules and crack his whip. Sometimes the skinner and his helper would jump down off the wagon and put their shoulders to the wheel to lighten the load and help the wagon come unstuck. The mules would pull and strain. If they could curse, they would probably curse the skinner!

For all his rough and rowdy ways our mule skinner still hopes to settle down one day. He hopes to find a woman who will "love him the best." He doesn't want to work in the wintertime. It's not easy hanging on to the reins when your fingertips are freezing. Anyway, he's not getting any younger.

In another traditional song ("The Ox-Driver's Song," anonymous), oxen were used to pull really heavy loads. He sings:

> I'll bid adieu to the whip and line,
> And drive no more in the wintertime.

RECOMMENDED LISTENING

These are variant versions of the song, entitled *Mule Skinner Blues.*
Bill Monroe, *Bean Blossom.* MCA 8002.
Hank Williams, Jr., *Living Proof.* Mercury 517320.

THE LONG LINE SKINNER BLUES

Lord, that - 'll love me best._____ See, pret - ty

See, pretty mama, pretty mama, look what you done done,
You made your daddy love you now your man done come.
I'm a long-line skinner and my home's out west,
Lookin' for the gal, Lord, that'll love me best.

I'm way down in the bottom skinning mules for Johnny Ryan,
Puttin' my initials, honey, on a mule's behind.
With my long whip line, babe. With my long whip line—
Lookin' for the woman who can ease my worried mind.

When the weather it gets chilly, gonna pack up my line,
'Cause I ain't skinnin' mules, Lord, in the wintertime.
Yes, I'm a long-line skinner and my home's out west,
And I'm lookin' for the woman, Lord, that'll love me the best.

The Midnight Special

The railroad train is a recurring subject in many black (and white) American folksongs, symbolizing freedom, escape, parting. There is the "Gospel Train" (like Michael's "gospel boat"), the "Union Train" (calling upon the workers to "get on board" and join the union), and the "Lonesome Train" (about Lincoln's funeral train).

We have already met John Henry, who "died with a hammer in his hand," digging the Big Bend Tunnel for the C. & O. line. We've been "down where the Southern cross' the Yellow Dog." We've followed Casey Jones on his fateful run down from Memphis that dark, rainy night.

Now we board the Golden Gate Limited, better known in song and story as the Midnight Special.

In 1873, Jay Gould (whom we met as one of the characters in the story of Casey Jones) was trying desperately to buy up the failing Texas & Pacific Railroad. He was "headed off at the pass" by an equally ruthless railroad speculator named Collis Huntington, whose dream (some called it a scheme) was to expand this line to link New Orleans to San Francisco, a distance of 2,489 miles (4,006 kilometers) of winding track: New Orleans, Houston, San Antonio, El Paso, Fort Yuma (Arizona), Los Angeles, San Francisco. By 1883 the Southern Pacific Railroad was in business all along the line.

The story of the Midnight Special begins at the Houston depot of the Southern Pacific.

Arriving from New Orleans, the train would pull out of the station at midnight, heading west. About 30 miles (48 kilometers) down the line from Houston was (and still is) the Texas State Prison Farm at Sugarland. The tracks pass within sight of the prison.

The black convicts, lying awake in their cells, would hear the lonesome whistle of the Midnight Special and, for a brief moment, the light from the locomotive would sweep past their windows.

The whistle and the light reminded the men of life beyond the walls of the prison. The Midnight Special became a symbol of that life, of freedom. Legends and tales grew up around the train. They said that

Huddie Ledbetter, known in musical circles as Leadbelly, the king of the twelve-string guitar, sang "The Midnight Special."

Prisoners worked in the cane fields under what was called the "convict leasing system," a practice that remained in effect until the early twentieth century.

if the headlight shone on a man as the train roared by, he would go free the next morning. They sang, "Let the Midnight Special shine her ever-lovin' light on me."

It is no accident that Sugarland, Texas, got to have such a sweet-sounding name. The fertile land of Fort Bend County was just right for growing sugarcane, as well as other crops. Large plantations and farms needed workers, and prison labor was cheap and plentiful. (For example, when Jay Gould was trying unsuccessfully to take over the Texas & Pacific Railroad in 1873, he rented black prison laborers from the state of Texas for a few cents a day. The master-slave mentality of the plantation owners had not been wiped out by the Civil War.)

Gangs of convicts would be sent out daily from the Sugarland Penitentiary to work the rich bottomland plantations. They toiled under the baking sun. The same men who sang and dreamed about the Midnight Special by night also sang another traditional prison song, "Shorty George."

> When I get back to Houston, I'm gonna walk and tell
> That the Fort Bend bottom is a burning hell.

Southern Pacific trains still leave the Houston Depot heading west, but the Golden Gate Limited—the Midnight Special—has long since been eliminated from the schedule. These days most people fly from Houston to San Francisco. The landing lights of the big jets don't shine through the windows of Sugarland.

▼▼▼

RECOMMENDED LISTENING

Leadbelly, *Folkways: The Original Vision.* Folkways/Smithsonian 40001.
Pete Seeger, *Live at Newport.* Vanguard 77008.

THE MIDNIGHT SPECIAL

Let___ the Mid - night Spe - cial___ shine her ev - er - lov - in' light on me.___

If you ever go to Houston, you'd better walk right,
And you better not stagger, and you better not fight.
'Cause the sheriff will arrest you and he'll carry you down,
And you can bet your bottom dollar you're Sugarland bound. *Chorus*

Yonder comes Miss Rosie, tell me how do you know?
I know her by her apron and the dress she wore.
Umbrella on her shoulder, piece of paper in her hand,
Well, I heard her tell the captain, "I want my man." *Chorus*

Lord, Thelma said she loved me, but I believe she told a lie,
'Cause she hasn't been to see me since last July.
She brought me little coffee, she brought me little tea.
She brought me nearly everything but the jail house key. *Chorus*

Well, the biscuits on the table, just as hard as any rock,
If you try to eat them, break a convict's heart.
My sister wrote a letter, my mother wrote a card,
"If you want to come to see us, you'll have to ride the rods." *Chorus*

I'm goin' away to leave you, and my time it ain't long.
The man is gonna call me, and I'm goin' home.
Then I'll be done all my grievin', whoopin', hollerin' and a-cryin';
Then I'll be done all my studyin' 'bout my great long time. *Chorus*

Don't You Leave Me Here

▼▼▼▼▼▼▼▼▼▼▼▼▼▼▼▼▼▼▼▼▼▼▼▼▼▼

> I thought I heard Buddy Bolden say,
> "You're nasty, you're dirty, take him away."

So run the opening words of "Buddy Bolden Blues," composed by Jelly Roll Morton as a tribute to the Buddy Bolden band, the first real jazz band. The nineteenth century was drawing to a close, Jelly Roll Morton was a young man, and Bolden was "king" of the cornet (to be followed by Freddie Keppard, Bunk Johnson, King Oliver, and Louis Armstrong).

Jelly Roll Morton was a "character," too good to be true. He claimed to have "invented" jazz. When a person makes a statement like that, whether it be true or false, we absolutely have to take a closer look at him.

Ferdinand Joseph La Menthe was born in New Orleans in 1885—or 1886 or 1888. He was always a little vague about dates. One thing is sure, he didn't want to be called "Frenchy," so he changed his name to Morton. The Jelly Roll was added on somewhere along the way. He grew up in the Latin, or French, Quarter of New Orleans, surrounded by the sounds of African, French, Spanish, Creole, and classical music that pulsated through the streets.

Morton himself was a Creole—of mixed black and European ancestry. French-Creole was his second language. Music was his first (along with English). By the time he was sixteen or seventeen he was already working as a pianist in the less-than-respectable establishments for which New Orleans was famous. At various times he also led a band, produced nightclub revues, managed nightclubs, and entertained on stage. All the while, Morton was composing songs and piano pieces in what he like to call the "latest style"—ragtime, blues, and jazz.

In 1902 he composed "New Orleans Blues." Years later (in 1938) he wrote: "It is evidently known, beyond contradiction, that

Jelly Roll Morton, the "inventor of jazz."

New Orleans is the cradle of jazz, and I, myself, happened to be the creator in the year 1902."[13]

It is very difficult to take such a claim seriously, since jazz, like any popular form of music, is the outgrowth of a collective effort of many musicians over a long period of time. However, in fairness to Morton, his early compositions and his style of piano playing did mark important milestones in the *development* of that music which came to be known as jazz.

His first big hit came in 1915 with the publication of a song in honor of himself, the "Jelly Roll Blues."

In New Orleans, in New Orleans, Louisiana town,
There's the finest boy for miles around.
Lord, Mister Jelly Roll, your affection he has stole.
What? No! I sho must say, babe,
You certainly can't abuse.
Isn't that a shame?
Don't you know that strain?
That's the Jelly Roll Blues.[14]

For the next thirty-six years, until his death in 1941, Morton continued composing, arranging, singing, playing his piano solos, and recording with his various bands. In 1938 he was invited to the Library of Congress by folklorist Alan Lomax to record his music and tell his story. He spent five weeks there—playing, singing, and reminiscing into the microphone. In response to the question, "Tell us who your folks were, where you were born . . .", Morton sat down at the piano and began to improvise:

As I can understand . . . my folks were in the city of New Orleans long before the Louisiana Purchase. . . . And all my folks directly from the shores of France . . . that is, across the world in the other world. . . . And they landed in the New World years ago. . . .[15]

Then he turned to Alan Lomax and said: "This is a little number I composed down in Alabama . . . around 1901 or 1902. The frequent saying was that any place you was going, you was bound for that place. So, in fact, I was Alabama bound."[16]

And this is the song he sang.

It contains a loosely joined series of "bluesy" verses that, rather than telling a continuous story, convey a feeling of dissatisfaction and wandering—typical blues themes.

▼▼▼

RECOMMENDED LISTENING

Jelly Roll Morton, *Centennial: His Complete Victor Recordings.*
RCA Bluebird 7361.
Jim Kweskin, *Troubadours of the Folk Era, Vol. 2.* Rhino 70263.

DON'T YOU LEAVE ME HERE

Words and Music adapted by Jelly Roll Morton

Don't you leave me here.___ Don't you

leave me here.___ If you just must

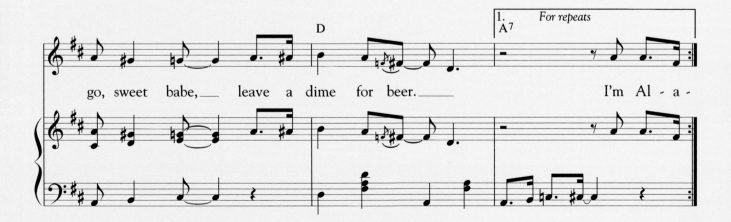

go, sweet babe,___ leave a dime for beer.___ I'm Al - a -

I'm Alabama bound,
I'm Alabama bound,
And if the train don't turn around,
I'm Alabama bound.

Oh, well your hair don't curl,
And your eyes ain't blue.
Well, if you don't want me, sweet Polly Ann,
Well, I don't want you.

Oh, don't you be like me,
Oh, don't you be like me,
Just drink your good wine every day,
And let the whisky be.

"Coda":
       Don't you leave me here…

The Darktown Strutter's Ball

▼▼▼▼▼▼▼▼▼▼▼▼▼▼▼▼▼▼▼▼▼▼▼▼▼▼▼▼▼▼▼▼▼▼▼▼

By 1917, when Shelton Brooks composed *The Darktown Strutters' Ball,* the black-inspired "jazz era" was in full swing. Record companies, recognizing the vast market for this exciting music, rushed to record black singers and bands. But this seemingly worthwhile decision ran smack into an an "unpleasant" fact of American life.

Except for the most superficial contacts, black and white people had very little to do with each other. In fact, the separation of the races, known as "segregation," virtually assured a second-rate citizenship to blacks. Schools, restaurants, theaters, public transportation—to mention just a few areas where blacks and whites might come together—were all strictly segregated, with an inferior quality of services reserved for blacks. The practice and custom of racial segregation were so ingrained that even record companies, which were all white-owned, felt obligated to issue these recordings in a special category, known as "race records." (Black and white musicians could not even appear together on stage in the same band until the 1930s.) The word "race" was a "polite" code word for "black" in those days.

Originally intended for black audiences, these race records were available for anyone to purchase, and millions of people—black and white—did just that, spreading jazz like wildfire across the nation and the world.

Black songwriters and composers such as Scott Joplin, W. C. Handy, and Jelly Roll Morton, among many others, saw their compositions easily crossing all racial barriers, even though they themselves still had to accept the many indignities that segregation imposed on them in their daily lives.

We have already briefly met Shelton Brooks, the composer of the 1913 hit song, "I Wonder Where My Easy Rider's Gone," which W. C. Handy drew upon in "Yellow Dog Blues." Brooks was born in Amesburg, Ontario, in 1886. You will remember that Canada was the northern terminus of the Underground Railroad, the escape route that slaves took to freedom before the Civil War.

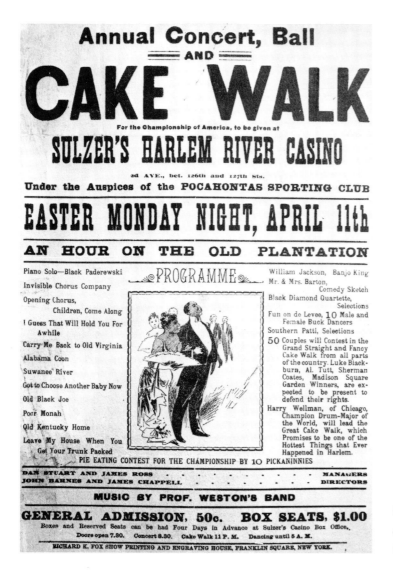

Cakewalking and other dance contests dated from slavery days and continued into the early twentieth century.

At an early age he moved to Detroit and began playing ragtime piano in local cafes. In 1910 he composed the song that put him on the map as a major figure in American popular music: "Some of These Days."

It was recorded and popularized for many years by Sophie Tucker, the daughter of Jewish immigrants, who was a star performer on the American musical scene for many years.

In addition to writing many successful songs, Brooks appeared in all-black musical shows, such as *Plantation Review* in 1922. He toured Europe in 1923 with *Blackbirds*, and appeared in *Dixie to Broadway* in 1924. All these shows have obvious "race" titles, in the sense of the

"race record" labels. They presented to white (and segregated) audiences a 1920s view of what was purported to be authentic black life. As dated as they may seem to us today, they were a historical step forward in the general acceptance of African–American culture beyond the black community itself.

Shelton Brooks outlived his contemporaries by many years. He died in California in 1975.

"The Darktown Strutters' Ball," which Brooks wrote in 1917, is another good example of a traditional "race" song that "crossed the line" to become an all-time hit.

Starting with the title itself, we are invited to "Darktown" (like

"Chinatown" or "Germantown," a district defined by its ethnic makeup). And what's happening in Darktown? Why, a ball, of course, "a very swell affair." Just as in Scott Joplin's "Ragtime Dance Song," the chance to dress up and step out becomes the focal point of the evening. He'll wear his "high silk hat and a frock-tail coat." She'll get all dolled up in her "Paris gown," and "new silk shawl."

Then comes the high point of the ball: "That fifty dollar prize, when we step out and 'Walk the Dog.'" "Walking the Dog" was a fancy dance step featured at cakewalking and other dance contests of the day.

To cap the evening's festivities, he's "Goin' to dance out both my shoes, When they play the 'Jelly Roll Blues.'" Yes . . . Jelly Roll Morton's "Jelly Roll Blues," which by this time was known to everybody. Just as Handy had drawn upon Brooks's *Wonder Where My Easy Rider's Gone,* Brooks here tips his hat to Jelly Roll.

▼▼▼

RECOMMENDED LISTENING

Count Basie, *Rock-A-Bye-Basie, Vol. 2.* Vintage Jazz Classics 1033.
Fats Waller, *Fats Waller.* RCA Special Products 1076.

THE DARKTOWN STRUTTERS' BALL

Words and Music by Shelton Brooks

1. I've got some good news, hon - ey, An in - vi - ta - tion to the
2. We'll meet our high - toned neigh - bors, An ex - hi - bi - tion of the

Dark - town Ball,___ It's a ver - y swell___ af - fair, All the
"Ba - by Dolls,"___ And each one will do___ their best, Just to

"High - brows" will be there.___ I'll wear my high silk hat and a
out - class all the rest.___ And there'll be dan - cers from ev - 'ry

frock - tail coat,___ You wear your Par - is gown, and your new silk shawl.___ There
for - eign land,___ The clas - sic, buck and wing, and the wood - en clog.___ We'll

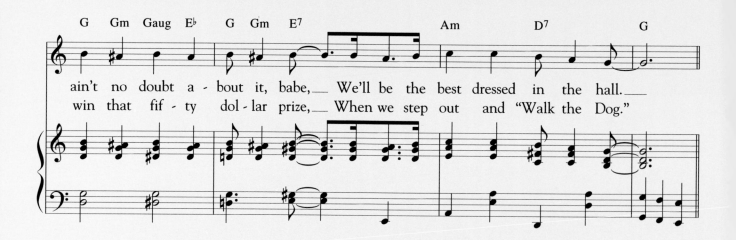

G   Gm Gaug E♭   G   Gm   E7   Am   D7   G

ain't no doubt a - bout it, babe,__ We'll be the best dressed in the hall.__

win that fif - ty dol - lar prize,__ When we step out and "Walk the Dog."

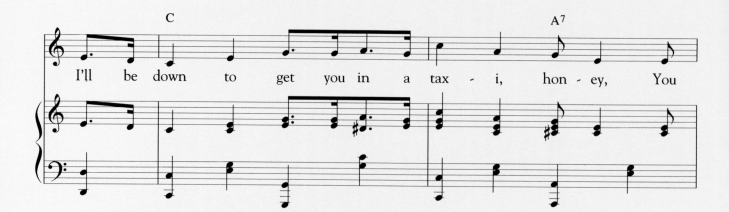

C   A7

I'll be down to get you in a tax - i, hon - ey, You

D7   G7

bet - ter be read - y a - bout half past eight.__ Now dear - ie,

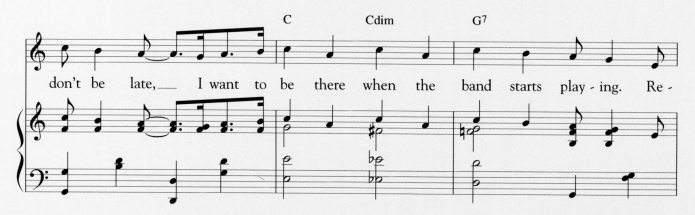

C   Cdim   G7

don't be late,__ I want to be there when the band starts play - ing. Re -

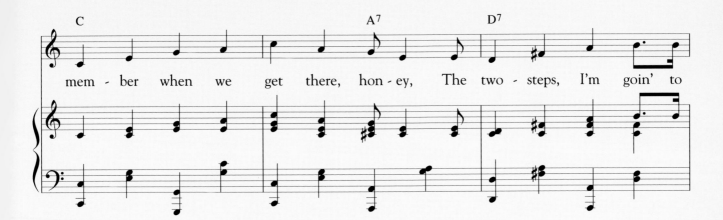

mem - ber when we get there, hon - ey, The two - steps, I'm goin' to

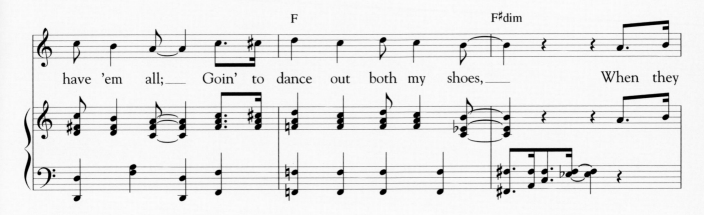

have 'em all;___ Goin' to dance out both my shoes,___ When they

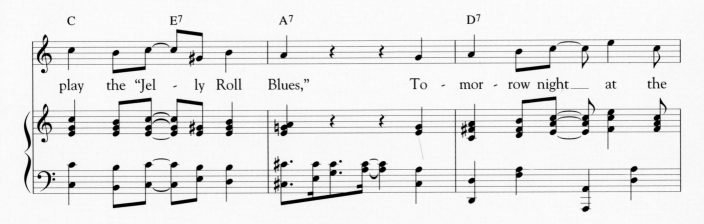

play the "Jel - ly Roll Blues," To - mor - row night___ at the

Dark - town Strut - ters' Ball.___

We Shall Overcome

On February 1, 1960, four black college students sat at a lunch counter in Greensboro, North Carolina, and asked for service. They were refused. From that single simple act grew a great movement of sit-ins at lunch counters and other public places, such as libraries, museums, beaches, and parks, that eventually resulted in the breaking down of racial segregation throughout the South.

It was not an easy task. The brave people who engaged in these sit-ins were often subjected to humiliation, violence, and arrest. But they persisted, and the conscience of the nation was aroused.

Theirs was a nonviolent movement. It was led by the Student Non-Violent Coordinating Committee (SNCC). Their weapon was solidarity. Their ammunition was song.

> Just listen to this song I'm singing, brother,
> You know it's true.
> If you're black and go to work for a living,
> This is what people will say:
> > If you're white—you're all right,
> > If you're brown—stick around,
> > But if you're black, oh brother,
> > Get back, get back, get back.[17]

This is a verse from "The Black, Brown and White Blues" by blues singer and guitarist William "Big Bill" Broonzy. It was written around 1946, when Broonzy observed that black soldiers returning from fighting for freedom around the world in the U.S. Army, in World War II, were still being discriminated against at home. He asks, "What's a black man got to do. . . ?" to be accepted as a man.

Broonzy was not alone in expressing his feelings against racial discrimination in song. Our country has a long tradition of protest songs on a great variety of subjects: slavery, women's rights, working conditions, war and peace—to name just a few.

One of the most powerful songs ever written on the subject of lynching (hanging of blacks by lawless mobs) in the South, is "Strange Fruit," composed in 1940 by a white man, Lewis Allen, and sung with great effect by jazz singer Billie Holiday and blues singer Josh White.

Blacks and whites banded together to exert political pressure for racial equality during the 1960s.

> Southern trees bear a strange fruit,
> Blood on the leaves and blood on the root.
> Black bodies hanging from magnolia trees.
> Strange fruit swinging in the southern breeze.[18]

So it was that when the student protesters realized and utilized the power of song to trumpet their message of equality for all in the 1960s, they were continuing a long and honorable tradition.

A whole body of freedom songs grew out of the sit-ins, voter registration campaigns, civil-rights rallies, and protest marches. They used the age-old method of writing new, up-to-date words to fit older, well-known tunes. Choruses were generally simple; after one hearing everybody could—and did—join in.

"We Shall Overcome" became the anthem of the freedom movement during the 1963 March on Washington led by Dr. Martin Luther King, Jr.

They sang at sit-ins. They sang at meetings. And, inevitably, they sang in jail. They sang,

> Deep in my heart, I do believe,
> We shall overcome some day.

"We Shall Overcome" is an adaptation of an old hymn, "I Shall Overcome." It became the musical symbol of the civil-rights movement, with its majestic melody and the ease with which new words could be added to fit ever-changing situations. Countless rallies, meetings, church services, and concerts ended with all present—black and white—linking arms and singing this powerful song.

▼▼▼

RECOMMENDED LISTENING

Because of its significance in the civil-rights movement,
"We Shall Overcome" has been recorded by many artists.
Here are just four fine performances.
Louis Armstrong, *What a Wonderful World.* RCA Bluebird 8310.
Mahalia Jackson, *Mahalia Jackson Sings Best Loved Hymns of
Dr. Martin Luther King.* Columbia 09686.
Peter, Paul and Mary, *Peter, Paul & Mommy, Too.* Warner Bros. 45216.
Pete Seeger, *We Shall Overcome.* Columbia 45312.

WE SHALL OVERCOME

Musical and Lyrical adaptation by Zilphia Horton, Frank Hamilton,
Guy Carawan and Pete Seeger. Inspired by African American Gospel
Singing, members of the Food & Tobacco Workers Union, Charleston, SC,
and the southern Civil Rights Movement.

TRO – © 1960 (Renewed 1988) and 1963 (Renewed 1991) Ludlow Music Inc,
New York, N.Y. Used by permission .
Royalties derived from this composition are being contributed to the We Shall
Overcome Fund and The Freedom Movement under the Trusteeship of the writers.

We are not afraid,
We are not afraid,
We are not afraid today.
Oh, deep in my heart, I do believe,
We shall overcome some day.

We are not alone…(today)…

The truth will make us free…(some day)…

We'll walk hand in hand…(today)…

The Lord will see us through…(today)…

Repeat first verse

Notes

▼▼▼

1. William Francis Allen, Charles Pickard Ware, and Lucy McKim Garrison, *Slave Songs of the United States,* 1867; reprint, New York: Oak Publications, 1965.
2. A resident of Johns Island, South Carolina, quoted in Guy Carawan and Candie Carawan, "John's Island: A Documentary in Picture, Song and Story." *Sing Out: The Folksong Magazine,* Vol. 16, No. 1, February–March 1966.
3. Allen, et al., *Slave Songs of the United States.*
4. Allen, et al., *Slave Songs of the United States.*
5. Between 1936 and 1938, the Federal Writers' Project Interviewed more than 6,000 former slaves, whose recollections of life before the Civil War were preserved in typewritten records entitled "Slave Narratives, A Folk History of Slavery in the United States from Interviews with Former Slaves." About 100 of these interviews were published in *Voices from Slavery,* edited by Norman Yetman (New York: Holt, Rinehart and Winston, 1970), from which this quotation is taken.
6. Yetman, *Voices From Slavery.*
7. Scott Joplin, *School of Ragtime,* 1908. Reprinted in Vera Brodsky Lawrence, *Scott Joplin Collected Piano Works* (New York Public Library, 1971).
8. Joplin, *School of Ragtime.*
9. W. C. Handy, *Father of the Blues: An Autobiography* (New York: Macmillan, 1955).
10. Handy, *Father of the Blues.*
11. Shelton Brooks, "I Wonder Where My Easy Rider's Gone," as quoted in *I Gotta Right to Sing the Blues* (Hasbro Heights, N.J.: Pearl Music, 1991).
12. Jelly Roll Morton, "Buddy Bolden's Blues," believed to have been written in 1902. Registered unpublished work (Washington D.C.: Tempo Music Pub. Co., 1939). Copyright assigned to Edward H. Morris, Inc. New York, 1968.
13. Alan Lomax, *Mister Jelly Roll* (New York: Grove Press, 1950).
14. Jelly Roll Morton, "Jelly Roll Blues," written in 1905. (Chicago, Ill.: Will Robsites, 1915).
15. Lomax, *Mister Jelly Roll.*
16. Lomax, *Mister Jelly Roll.*
17. William "Big Bill" Broonzy, "The Black, Brown, and White Blues," written in 1945, copyright 1946. First published in "People Songs." Vol. 1, No. 10, November 1946.
18. Lewis Allen, "Strange Fruit," copyright 1940 by Edward B. Marks Music Corp., New York.

Further Reading

Blesh, Rudi. *Shining Trumpets: A History of Jazz.* New York: Knopf, 1946.

Blesh, Rudi, and Harriet Janis. *They All Played Ragtime.* New York: Oak Publications, 1966.

Botkin, B. A., and Alvin F. Harlow. *A Treasury of Railroad Folklore.* New York: Crown, 1953.

Handy, W. C. *Father of the Blues: An Autobiography.* New York: Macmillan, 1955.

Haskins, James. *Scott Joplin: The Man Who Made Ragtime.* New York: Stein and Day, 1980.

Lomax, Alan. *Mister Jelly Roll.* New York: Grove, 1950.

Ramsey, Frederic, Jr., and Charles Edward Smith, eds. *Jazzmen.* New York: Harcourt, Brace, 1939.

SONG BOOKS AND MUSIC COLLECTIONS WITH HISTORICAL NOTES

Carawan, Guy, and Candie Carawan, compilers. *We Shall Overcome! Songs of the Southern Freedom Movement.* New York: Oak Publications, 1963.

Dapogny, James, ed. *Ferdinand "Jelly Roll" Morton: The Collected Piano Music.* Washington, D.C.: Smithsonian Institution Press, 1982.

Handy, W. C., ed. *Blues: An Anthology. 53 Songs by W. C. Handy.* With a historical and critical text by Abbie Niles; revised by Jerry Silverman. New York: Macmillan, 1972.

Lawrence, Vera Brodsky, ed. *Scott Joplin: Collected Piano Works.* New York: The New York Public Library, 1971.

————. *Scott Joplin's Treemonisha.* New York: Chappell Music Co., 1975.

Schlein, Irving, ed. *Slave Songs of the United States.* New York: Oak Publications, 1965. Reprint of 1867 collection.

Silverman, Jerry. *Ballads & Songs of the Civil War.* Pacific, Mo.: Mel Bay Publications, 1993.

————. *Blues Classics Songbook.* Pacific, Mo.: Mel Bay Publications, 1993.

————. *Folk Blues.* New York: Macmillan, 1958. Republished in 1983 by Saw Mill Music.

————. *The Ragtime Songbook.* Pacific, Mo.: Mel Bay Publications, 1990. (with cassette)

————. *Traditional Black Music.* (15 volumes). New York: Chelsea House, 1992–1995.

MUSIC INSTRUCTION

Silverman, Jerry: *How to Play Blues Guitar.* New York: Saw Mill Music, 1982.

————. *How to Play Ragtime Guitar.* New York: Saw Mill Music, 1982.

Index

▼▼▼

About the Author

▼▼▼

Jerry Silverman is a professional folksinger and guitarist. He has devoted his time and considerable talent to teaching and performing in schools all over the country. Since publishing his first songbook in 1958, he has written more than one hundred books, including many well-known method books for the guitar. Many of his titles are songbooks organized around international and American themes. His most recent Millbrook title is *Songs and Stories from the American Revolution.*

Silverman lives in Hastings-on-Hudson, New York.